DELACROIX

MASTERS AND MOVEMENTS

LEE JOHNSON

DELACROIX

W. W. NORTON & COMPANY, INC.
NEW YORK

ACKNOWLEDGEMENTS

I wish to thank M. Germain Bazin and members of his staff too numerous to mention individually, for enabling me to examine and photograph the paintings by Delacroix in the Louvre under the best possible conditions; Mme Bouchot-Saupique and M. Maurice Sérullaz, who with unfailing courtesy accorded me like facilities in the Cabinet des dessins; the curators of other museums, the collectors and dealers who have supplied photographs of works in their care or possession and given permission to reproduce them; Sir Anthony Blunt, Douglas Cooper and Jack Goodison for encouragement and criticism in the various phases of my research; Stephen Rees Jones and Dr Robert Ratcliffe for much illuminating discussion on nineteenth-century colour theory and practice.

My initial researches into Delacroix's use of colour were aided by a grant from the Research Fund of the University of London. In addition to this grant, I gratefully acknowledge funds for travelling received from the Courtauld Institute, King's College, Cambridge, and the University of Toronto.

'What is Romanticism?', asks Baudelaire; and he replies: 'modern art'. Delacroix, he says, had been proclaimed leader of the modern school by the public since the exhibition of his first work. How then is he modern? What specific quality makes him the 'true painter of the nineteenth century'? According to Baudelaire, it is the 'singular and persistent melancholy that emanates from all his works'. Remove this link, says the poet, and the whole chain of history would be broken.

Although Delacroix distrusted the label 'Romantic', preferring to think of himself as a modern propagator of the classical tradition, he once conceded in his maturity that he had always been a Romantic, if by his Romanticism one meant 'the free manifestation' of his 'personal impressions', his 'distaste for the types invariably copied in the art schools' and his 'loathing for academic recipes'. In spite of his habitual reluctance to accept it, the title of leader of the French Romantic School conferred on him by his contemporaries must stand. Unlike his academic rival Ingres, Delacroix was not the father of any school and professed no rigid doctrine; he was simply the greatest of the Romantic figure painters — indeed the only major master — and in this sense their leader. He was Romantic not only in the general sense that he defines and in the special quality defined by Baudelaire, but in his preference for subjects drawn from mediaeval or Renaissance history (Pls. 20, 32, 33, 35) over those inspired by classical history (David) or stirring contemporary episodes in the history of France (David, Gros and Géricault). Romantic too was his habit of deriving inspiration from mediaeval, Renaissance and contemporary rather than classical writers. His chief literary sources were Shakespeare (Pls. 36, 55), Byron (Pls. 13, 14, 30, 54), and

Walter Scott (Pl. 18). Other authors who inspired pictures by him were Dante (Pl. 4), Ariosto (Pl. 57), Tasso, Robert Burns (Pl. 53), Chateaubriand (Pl. 6), Goethe (Pls. 11, 58) and Charles Maturin (Pl. 21). Delacroix often treated classical themes too, especially in later maturity, but when he did, it was with a melancholy, a lyricism or an animation that in contrast to the measured frigidity of the Neo-Classicists mark him as essentially Romantic (Pls. 40, 41, 42, 47, 70).

If all these characteristics are fundamental to an appreciation of Delacroix's work within the context of his period, it is yet true that all but those enumerated by Delacroix himself could be ignored and the continuity of the history of art would not be seriously weakened. For Courbet and Manet virtually put an end to the development of Delacroix's type of melancholy and subject matter; and though two precious jewels — Moreau and Redon — dangle from it, the link wrought by Baudelaire has no connection with the major chain of development in nineteenth-century French painting after the death of Delacroix. Yet Cézanne is reported to have said, speaking for himself and his famous contemporaries: ' We are all in Delacroix '; and he planned to paint an *Apotheosis of Delacroix*. Monet, Renoir, Seurat, Gauguin, Van Gogh all admired Delacroix's work and were influenced by it. Not one of these painters in his maturity continued the literary and historical themes or melancholy sentiment of Delacroix. What attracted them to him was, above all, his use of colour. He was the supreme colourist of the first half of the nineteenth century and for this very reason somewhat isolated from and at variance with his contemporaries. Now the primary distinction of all these masters of the latter half of the century was their brilliant handling of colour. None of their immediate predecessors could have taught them so much about colour as Delacroix. It seems to be time therefore, one hundred years after Delacroix's death, to try and replace, or rather strengthen, Baudelaire's link by reviewing Delacroix's develpment in relation to his colour theory and practice, and re-assessing what these owe to tradition, how far they may be original, what their connection was with the future.

Baudelaire recognized the central importance of colour in Delacroix's style, though he could not foresee its full significance for the future. He stresses his ability to evoke mood by means of colour. Delacroix himself says that colour should be adapted to the mood of the subject in painting, but gives no indication in his writings of the specific sentiments he associates with any given colours. There is nevertheless a clear correspondence between mood and choice of colour in many of his works (Pls. 4, 30, 55). Delacroix also observed that colour has a purely abstract or, as he called it, ' musical ' quality that exists independently of the subject depicted. One could, he felt, be affected by the harmony of a painting in the abstract before being near enough to it to recognize the subject. He often exploits this quality; in a painting he will use touches of colour which are arbitrary from a representational point of view, and whose sole function is not to represent something as it would appear in nature, nor to evoke a specific emotion, but to enhance the chromatic harmony as a thing apart. This, then, is one major feature of Delacroix's use of colour: a use that is not descriptive, but emotive, expressive or absolute in itself. Colour that is intended either to arouse certain emotions relative to a theme or simply to create a pictorial feast for the eye. If the idea was not entirely new, the emphasis Delacroix laid on it in conversation, in his writings and pictures assumes a special significance in the light of later developments.

Baudelaire inclines to be sublimely elusive when writing of the other aspect of Delacroix's handling of colour: the naturalistic, analytic, rational or scientific application of colour. Other nineteenth century writers, notably the art historians Charles Blanc and Théophile Silvestre and the Neo-Impressionist painter Paul Signac, deal more explicitly, though scarcely more accurately, with this side of Delacroix's style. They seem to overestimate or misinterpret the influence of contemporary scientific thought on Delacroix, and they underrate the importance of his own direct observation of nature joined to constant study of how the Old Masters reproduced the colours in nature. To the present day, the high degree of realism in Delacroix's colour has been obscured by the nature of his subject matter, and consequently it is the influence of Courbet and the Barbizon School on the Impressionists that has been stressed. In fact, Delacroix is in every respect a more progressive colourist than Courbet, and the realistic colour principles that he applies to subjects far removed from contemporary reality are of more profound consequence to Impressionism than the techniques of either Courbet or the Barbizon painters.

The problem of scientific influence on Delacroix's colour theory and practice cannot be fully solved from the evidence at present available. Delacroix had an unscientific, indeed anti-scientific, temperament. In spite of this, it is clear that some of his technical devices are influenced by contemporary scientific thought; and, particularly in later life, he observed colours in nature in a way that would not have been possible before certain basic scientific truths concerning the composition of light had been widely diffused in the nineteenth century. Wherever the precise limits of the influence of science on Delacroix may eventually prove to lie, it is at least certain that the interpretation of this influence by writers such as Charles Blanc did much to inspire the scientific experiments with colour of Van Gogh and the Neo-Impressionists.

The two leading characteristics of Delacroix's handling of colour correspond in some measure to the two sides of his personality, which was on the one hand intuitive, impetuous, febrile, naïve, and on the other, rational, sceptical, sophisticated, aloof. The former traits were the more innate and those which Delacroix valued most as an artist; the latter were more the product of educatian and disappointment, though with time Delacroix came to prize them almost as highly as the others. He soon learnt that in the world one often succeeds more, as he put it, ' *avec le savoir-faire qu'avec le véritable savoir* ', and, being ambitious, he taught himself to dissimulate, with all but his most intimate friends, the deeper and more impulsive aspects of his character beneath a veneer of reasoned diplomacy and social charm. Baudelaire likens him to the ' crater of a volcano artistically concealed by bouquets of flowers '. So successfully indeed did

Plate I - Female Nude, c. 1820. ▶

Plate 2 - PORTRAIT OF AN OLD WOMAN, c. 1822-6.

Plate 3 - NEREID, copied from Rubens' LANDING OF MARIA DE' MEDICI AT MARSEILLES, c. 1822.

Plate 4 - Barque de Dante, Salon 1822.

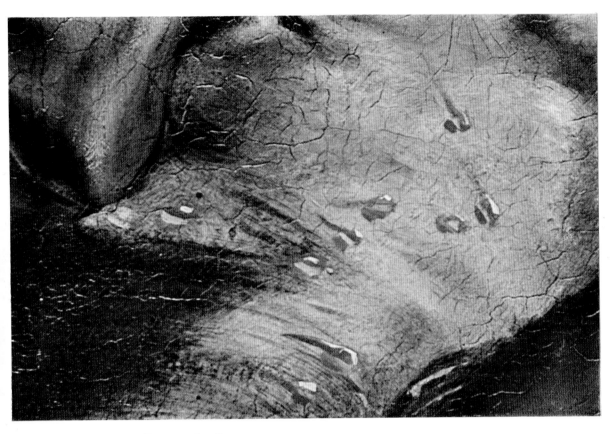

Plate 5 - BARQUE DE DANTE, detail.

Plate 6 - THE NATCHEZ, begun 1823, Salon 1835.

Plate 7 - HEAD OF A WOMAN, study for the MASSACRE DE SCIO, 1824. ▶

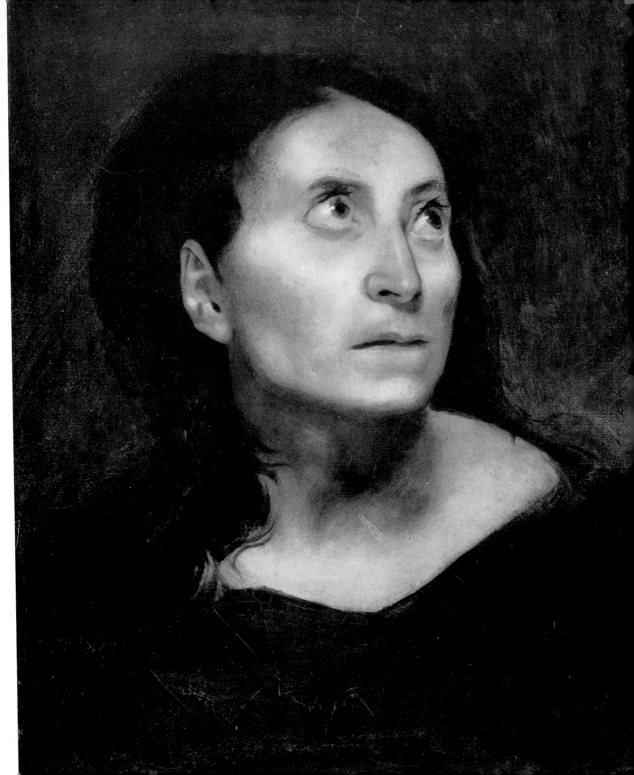

Plate 8 - MASSACRE DE SCIO, Salon 1824.

he disguise his volcanic nature, that he was much sought after in Parisian society during the July Monarchy and Second Empire. He became renowned for his brilliant and witty conversation, which was more generally appreciated than his painting. His friend George Sand attempted to capture some of its savour in her *Impressions et Souvenirs*, but the best written record of Delacroix's lively, cultivated spirit is the Journal, which he kept from 1822-24 and from 1847 to his death in 1863. In a lucid, informal style, he records his day-to-day reflections on painting, music, literature, the theatre, history, contemporary politics and personalities, and many lesser topics. His wide knowledge of history and the arts of all periods always informs his trenchant judgments of contemporary developments in politics and the arts; he combines historical perspective with strongly expressed personal views in an exceptionally stimulating way. Possessing a flexible and constantly developing intelligence, Delacroix never fears to change his mind, to contradict himself, to record an incomplete and random thought or a wild prejudice. If there is much truth in his quip that Ingres' work is the 'complete expression of an incomplete intellect', it is equally true that his own writings and to some extent his paintings are the incomplete expression of a complete intelligence. Whereas Ingres is all but perfect within the limits he set himself and tried to impose on others, thus leaving little room for development, Delacroix is full of imperfections and incompletely realized ideas, but, having prescribed no limits to the artistic spirit, allowed ample play for future growth. His art and writings contain enough fruitful suggestions and flashes of intuition to have inspired generations of painters.

After receiving a classical education at the *Lycée Impérial* (now *Louis-le-Grand*) in Paris, followed by a Neo-Classical training in the studio of Guérin, Delacroix opened his public career at the age of twenty-four with the *Barque de Dante* (Pl. 4), which he exhibited at the Salon of 1822. The picture is Romantic in its subject, inspired by Canto VIII of Dante's *Inferno*, in its lugubrious mood, in the emphasis on the torment of damned souls. In other respects it remains within the academic Neo-Classical tradition founded by David:

in the arrangement of the composition in planes parallel to the surface of the canvas, in the sculptural quality of the nudes, in the impression they convey, in spite of a certain Romantic energy deriving mainly from Michelangelo and Rubens, of having been separately studied and posed individually to impress an academic Salon jury. Sculptural though they are, they are freely handled in a bold impasto in contrast to the marmoreal finish of nudes by David and his most gifted pupil Ingres, who taught that painting should be sculptural and should never reveal the touch of the brush. In colour and technique the flesh passages are very closely related to those in the *Raft of the Medusa* (Louvre. Salon 1819) by Géricault who, with Gros, was the chief contemporary influence on the early Delacroix. Delacroix employs the same Caravaggesque chiaroscuro, the same ochreish and leaden tones, the same dense black, dark olive or brown shadows. It is a sculptural and tonal, not colouristic, manner of modelling in that form is constructed by means of opaque pigment and sharp contrasts of tone rather than by subtle variations of hue.

Partly academic the *Barque de Dante* may be, but so powerful is the design, so compelling the plastic force of the figures, that it was to become a model for progressive painters as important as plaster casts were to academics. It was copied by Courbet, Manet, Degas, Cézanne, Gauguin and a multitude of lesser painters.

The one place where Delacroix seems to make a significant advance in the use of colour is in the drops of water on some of the figures in the foreground: they are composed of juxtaposed touches of pure pigments (Pl. 5). Pierre Andrieu, Delacroix's pupil and his chief assistant from 1850 to the master's death, reports that Delacroix told him these drops of water were his starting point as a colourist. He says that they originated from observing the rainbow and from studying the nereids in Rubens' *Landing of Maria de' Medici at Marseilles* (Louvre), one of which Delacroix copied about 1822 (Pl. 3). Delacroix greatly intensifies, and by the addition of green increases the range of, the colours in the drops of water on Rubens' nereids. He may have been induced to make these changes by observation of the rainbow. But however he arrived at the final effect, the analytical principle he applies of dividing into pure coloured components an object that to the average eye would appear monochrome or colourless, is of far-reaching significance for the future. Later Delacroix was to extend the same principle to the painting of figures, and eventually with Impressionism the system was to spread over entire landscapes and festive open-air figure paintings, resulting in one of the richest flowerings of colour since the Venetian Renaissance.

The *Barque de Dante* was relatively well received in academic circles and acquired by the State. With his second and much larger Salon painting, the *Massacre de Scio* (Pl. 8), which more surprisingly was also purchased by the State, Delacroix opened the breach between official teaching, dominated by the ideas of David, and progressive painters. This breach was continuously widened by Delacroix then by Courbet, and ended in total rupture in the Impressionist era. The subject of the *Massacre* is contemporary, an episode from the current Greek War of Independence, but characteristically Romantic in the opportunity it affords for a display of liberal sympathies mingled with rape and bloodshed among exotic characters in picturesque costumes — tasteless by academic standards, and far too loosely executed. Yet the frieze-like arrangement of the principal figures evinces a continuing debt to David; and there is a precedent for this type of colourful Near-Eastern scene of suffering in the *Plague at Jaffa* (Louvre. Salon 1804) by David's pupil Gros. But Gros included the heroic presence of Napoleon to compensate for any lapses of taste. There are no unalloyed heroes in Delacroix's picture. The Greeks are no more heroic than the screaming women in Picasso's *Guernica* and far more passive, the Turks no less heroic than the bull in the same painting. If Delacroix's sympathy for the Greeks were not recorded elsewhere, he might be suspected of favouring the Turkish cause, for in this painting, as so often later, he is at his most forceful in depicting the vital powers of destruction, and the passive submission of the weak seems but a foil magnifying the relentless atrocity of these powers.

Delacroix set to work on the final canvas of the *Massacre de Scio* on 12th January 1824. It was exhibited at the Salon in the same year. In his Journal Delacroix reveals a desire to break with the aggressive plasticity and somewhat academic enumeration of muscles in the *Barque de Dante*: his major preoccupation now seems to be to combine clear-cut contour with simple internal modelling composed of a 'firm yet blended impasto'. He finds these qualities not in the colourists, but in Raphael, Ingres, in some works by Géricault, and in a seventeenth-century Spanish portrait that he was copying, believing it to be a Velasquez. His solution can be seen in a study for the *Massacre de Scio* (Pl. 7) and in the majority of figures in the completed painting: firmly accented contours, smoothly blended tonal impasto with little complication of detail and unrelieved by brightly coloured hatchings.

As late as 7th May, when the whole *Massacre de Scio* had been blocked in and most of the figures were well advanced, Delacroix records in his Journal that he wishes it to contain '*ce bon noir, cette heureuse saleté*' that he admired in the Spanish portrait. Reports from other sources also suggest that in the initial stages large areas of the painting were, as indeed some of them remain, dark and drab in tone. It must nevertheless be assumed that from the beginning Delacroix established his major colour harmony, which is based on the blue and orange-yellow of the sky, repeated with variations in the blue skirt of the principal female figure in the lefthand group and the orange drapery of the old woman in the other group. But there is good reason to believe that in spite of this broad harmony, the picture lacked a more delicate unity of light and atmosphere.

Then on 19th June Delacroix notes that he has seen some works by Constable and that they did him a 'great deal of good'. Six days later he saw them again. They were a group of paintings on view at a Parisian dealer's gallery, two of which, *The Hay Wain* and *View on the Stour*, were to be hung at the Salon of 1824. Delacroix writes nothing of the influence of Constable on the *Massacre de Scio*, nor does he make any explicit reference to the evolution of the painting after 18th June; but other sources testify that he retouched it after seeing the Constables. They disagree as to the exact nature of the retouching and the time when it was done. Théophile

Plate 9 - MASSACRE DE SCIO, detail.

Plate 10 - PORTRAIT OF THE SINGER BAROILHET (?) IN TURKISH COSTUME, c. 1826.

Plate II - Faust in his Study, c. 1826.

Plate 12 - BRIGHTON. WORTHING IN THE DISTANCE, 1825.

Silvestre, with whom Delacroix is known to have discussed the impression made on him by Constable while he was painting the *Massacre de Scio*, states, in a book published during the artist's lifetime, that the picture was retouched in the Louvre before the opening of the Salon — on 25th August. Probably the most reliable account of the nature of the retouching is given by Andrieu in an essay edited by Silvestre, which has hitherto been disregarded in discussions of the Constable problem. Andrieu quotes Delacroix as saying that he retouched the *Massacre de Scio* during the fortnight before the opening of the Salon, using the brightest colours on his palette and recalling his starting point, the drops of water in the *Barque de Dante*. Frédéric Villot, Delacroix's friend from about 1830, claims that Delacroix said in connexion with the retouching that if it was necessary to begin a painting with a broom, it must be finished with a needle.

It was one of Constable's major contributions to modern painting that he made every part of his landscapes partake of the light of the sky, by scattering them with minute, vibrant particles of paint. He thus introduced a unity of flickering light and atmosphere, which from all indications is precisely what the *Massacre de Scio* was lacking. Closer inspection of the old woman in Delacroix's picture shows her arm, prepared in the colourless fashion of the study for this figure, to be covered with small hatchings of pink, orange-yellow and pale blue — applied, so to speak, with a ' needle ' (Pl. 9). Touches of pure green and red, similar in size and colour to touches in the drops of water of the *Barque de Dante*, are placed in the flat brown shadow at the elbow. Orange particles and rarer dots of blue are flecked over the skirt; colour apart, the former are exactly like the dry, broken crumbs of impasto that add the sparkle of reflected light to trees and fields and water in Constable's *Hay Wain*. Similarly, the whole sandy foreground of Delacroix's painting is enlivened with small patches of orange-yellow and blue, applied over rougher brushwork swept in with a ' broom '. And the dull shadow on the infant at his dead mother's breast is lightly speckled with blue and orange dots.

Unless new evidence comes to light, general agreement on the precise limits of the retouching may never be reached; it is likely that it was mostly concentrated in the foreground where it would have been most apparent to visitors to the Salon. But if the small, brightly coloured touches that have been indicated are admitted to have been inspired by Constable, then the meaning of his influence is clear. They serve to scatter, not the ' cool tint of English daylight ' as do Constable's less variegated touches, but the bright hues of a Mediterranean sky; they introduce colour and transparency into dark shadows; and they help to bind separately studied passages into a subtly animated chromatic harmony. Delacroix's innovation is to have used a generally wider range of spectral hues for his touches and to have applied them to a monumental figure painting instead of to landscape.

Delacroix did not immediately pursue his experiments with Constable's type of technique, but the final touches in the *Massacre de Scio* are allied to his later concept of ' *liaison* ', which he defines as ' that air, those reflections which form a whole of objects the most disparate in colour '. Two ultimate developments from the treatment of the foreground in the *Massacre de Scio* seem possible: either the impulsively slashed blue and orange hatchings which constitute the foreground of a *Sower* by Van Gogh from the Arles period (Kröller-Müller Museum, Otterlo); or the meticulous division into minute coloured components, based on scientific study of the composition of light, of sections of the foreground in Seurat's *Sunday Afternoon on the Grande Jatte* (Art Institute, Chicago). It is not necessary to claim a direct influence of the *Massacre de Scio* on these passages (although parts of the foreground of the *Grande Jatte*, sprinkled with scattered dots of celestial blue and solar orange, are no more ' scientifically ' handled than Delacroix's foreground); but it seems important to recognize Delacroix's retouching as a possible beginning of the historical process that led to them. Under the influence of Constable, he had made a new departure by breaking with the brittle, airless handling of the Neo-Classical school as represented by his master Guérin, of whose *Aeneas and Dido* (Louvre. Salon 1817) the Scottish painter Andrew Robertson had complained: ' the landscape is very indifferent, and like the drapery of Dido does not partake of the colour of the sky '.

From the end of May 1825 Delacroix spent about three months in England where he came in touch mainly with British portrait and history painters, meeting Lawrence, Wilkie and Etty. Though he seems to have had fewer relationships with the leading English landscape painters, he did a fair number of watercolours from nature in England which reveal a strong English influence (Pl. 12). In his figure paintings immediately following the English journey there is a marked increase in the use of rich glazes that can be largely attributed to English influence (Pls. 10, 13, 14, 17). Since the eighteenth century, English figure painters had continued to employ glazes to obtain sonorous effects of colour, whereas orthodox French Neo-Classicists, in reaction against Rococo techniques, appear to have regarded extensive glazing as a sign of technical incompetence.

It may also be the result of English influence in 1825 that in the four years following his return to France, three of Delacroix's major history paintings were to be inspired by English literature: *The Murder of the Bishop Liège*, from Walter Scott's *Quentin Durward* (Pl. 18); the *Execution of Marino Faliero*, from a play by Byron (Pl. 13); and the *Death of Sardanapalus*, also inspired by one of Byron's plays (Pl. 14). The *Bishop of Liège* not only depicts an incident from English literature, but has a setting inspired by Westminster Hall and contains apparent reminiscences of Wilkie's oil sketch for *John Knox Preaching before the Lords of the Congregation* (Petworth House), a sketch which Delacroix had seen and admired in Wilkie's studio. In both pictures the principal heretic, square-faced and bearded, is placed on the far right beneath a canopy, and in both his forceful gesture motivates the reactions of the group on the left, which includes a bishop with mitre and crozier.

The *Death of Sardanapalus*, as large as the *Massacre de Scio*, was exhibited at the Salon of 1827. In its militant Romanticism it is as provocative a manifesto of the Romantic revolt against Neo-Classical constriction as Victor Hugo's Preface to *Cromwell* of the same year. The King of Nineveh, his palace besieged by rebellious subjects, has ordered the slaughter of his entire retinue, who are piled with the royal treasures on his funeral pyre. The *Sardanapalus*, with its luminous diagonal thrusting from lower right to upper left, its exuberance of colour and movement, is the most Baroque of Delacroix's major paintings to date and owes the most to Rubens, who with Veronese was the Old Master to have the greatest influence on Delacroix. But more than traces of Neo-Classical influence remain: the composition is partly based on an engraving of a pseudo-Etruscan relief depicting a scene of slaughter, which accounts for the uncomfortable tension between the Baroque diagonal in depth and the frieze-like disposition of horse and figures foiled by the steeply tilted foreground. Later, Delacroix was to resolve this tension between Baroque and Neo-Classical methods of composition. In a *Christ on the Sea of Galilee* of the 1850s, for example, he retains the Baroque diagonal, but counteracts its recession by tilting the whole composition (not merely the foreground as in the *Sardanapalus*) into an almost vertical plane, and by placing limbs, oars and draperies parallel to the picture plane along the entire length of the diagonal (Pl. 65).

Of the *Sardanapalus*, which owes so much to Rubens, Delacroix might have complained in his maturity, as he did of a work by the Baroque master: ' It is like an assembly where everyone speaks at the same time '. But he was also tolerant of his youthful extravagances and might have added another remark that he applied to Rubens: ' *La force, la véhémence, l'éclat le dispensent de la grâce et du charme* '. Rubens, he thought, was for all his faults truly Homeric whereas Ingres, whose *Apotheosis of Homer* was exhibited at the same Salon as the *Sardanapalus*, was Homeric ' only in pretension '. Delacroix defined the Homeric quality as ' the true cry of suffering, the sweat of the fighter or of the labourer, the atrocious detail often carried to an extreme, the blood, the tears, which make us men '. The attainment in painting of this quality, which when found in the nineteenth century we define as ' Romantic ', was one way in which Delacroix felt he came closer to the true spirit of antiquity than had David and Ingres, whom he considered frigid antiquarians. Rubens helped him to attain it in the *Sardanapalus*, but it is important too that the basic framework of the composition and several of the poses were derived from an engraving of a relief that would have been

Plate 13 - EXECUTION OF MARINO FALIERO, 1826, Salon 1827. ▶

Plate 14 - DEATH OF SARDANAPALUS, Salon 1827-8.

Plate 15 - Study for DEATH OF SARDANAPALUS.

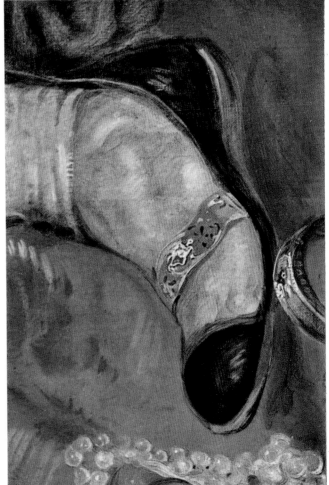

Plate 16 - DEATH OF SARDANAPALUS, detail.

Plate 17 - HEAD OF A WOMAN, c. 1827, probably Salon 1827.

Plate 18 - MURDER OF THE BISHOP OF LIÈGE, 1829, Salon 1831.

Plate 19 - LIBERTY LEADING THE PEOPLE, 1830, Salon 1831.

Plate 20 - BATTLE OF POITIERS, 1830.

Plate 21 - INTERIOR OF A DOMINICAN CONVENT IN MADRID: AN INCIDENT FROM
« MELMOTH THE WANDERER », 1831, Salon 1834.

approved of as a source by the most orthodox Neo-Classicist. Thus Delacroix, far from renouncing the Neo-Classical methods in which he had been instructed, transforms them by the introduction of Baroque elements to create a truly Romantic masterpiece, which he would probably have thought of as Homeric, and therefore more truly classical than the works of David or Ingres.

The classical elements in the *Christ on the Sea of Galilee* (arrangement parallel to the picture plane, at least one gesture borrowed from the Antique) are less obvious precisely because they are more completely fused with the Baroque characteristics. Géricault, in his *Raft of the Medusa*, had attempted a similar fusion of Baroque and classical styles and Romantic sentiment. Delacroix dispenses with Géricault's clanking mechanics and has resolved the discords of style in his own *Sardanapalus*, creating a fully modern painting — modern in the disregard for conventional illusionistic perspective, in the deliberate use of spatial ambiguities and distortions of anatomy for purely pictorial ends.

According to Andrieu, Delacroix wished to reproduce the variety of hue and the blond tonality of pastels in the *Sardanapalus*, and his statement has been vindicated by the recent discovery of a group of pastel studies for this painting (Pl. 15). Delacroix succeeds best in translating his pastel technique into oils in the foot of the male slave in the right foreground (Pls. 15, 16). First, he lays in evenly the general tone of the flesh, corresponding to the buff paper in the pastel study, then without obscuring this preparation with opaque layers of impasto he goes over it with delicate, multi-coloured hatchings, which bring the foot into relief; having started by placing the rainbow in a drop of water, he now spreads it diaphanously over a whole foot. Depending entirely on colour relationships and direction of stroke to create an illusion of solidity, this technique is the antithesis of the sculptural method of modelling. It is one of the many small passages in a work by Delacroix where he seems to adumbrate much in the future course of French painting, but surrounds it with the encumbrances of the Grand Manner, of which he was the last exponent, and the theatrical trappings of Romanticism.

The colour scheme as a whole is imaginative in essence. Delacroix is not concerned here with a naturalistic unifying atmosphere, or with easing the transition from one bright colour to another by reproducing realistically exchanges of coloured reflections. Had the picture been painted twenty years later, he would, for instance, almost certainly have placed pink reflections from the bedspread in the back of the nude leaning against the couch on the right, as they would exist in reality. But it was the pageant alone that concerned him in 1827, the splendid feast for the eye. It is interesting in this connexion that a contemporary critic should have compared the *Sardanapalus* to a Persian carpet and the amalgam of colours in a kaleidoscope. For Delacroix in his turn is reported by Maxime du Camp to have said later that the most beautiful pictures he had seen were certain Persian carpets. And finally, Gauguin, an immediate forerunner of abstract painting, having probably read du Camp, used the analogy of a Persian carpet in describing the abstract quality of a *Self-portrait* he had painted for Van Gogh.

For his next Salon Delacroix turned from the remote agonies of ancient Assyrian history to paint his only major work inspired by a contemporary historical event in France: *Liberty Leading the People* (Pl. 19), a tribute to the insurgents of the July Revolution of 1830. Exceptional in subject, the picture does not belong, either, in the main progression of Delacroix's development as a colourist: treating a topical realistic theme, Delacroix returns for the most part to the earthy palette of Géricault. It is however characteristic of him rather than of Géricault to introduce a literary element in the form of the allegorical figure of Liberty. She has been repeatedly compared to a *femme du peuple* since the nineteenth century. The comparison may be apt, but it implies a kind of realism that was alien to Delacroix even in a theme of this sort; and it should also be pointed out that the Liberty appears to be a free and lively variation of the *Aphrodite of Melos*, which was discovered in 1820 and first exhibited in the Louvre the following year.

The figure wearing a top hat has often been said to be a self-portrait, but it little resembles Delacroix as he is known from portraits and daguerreotypes, and in any event he did not fight in the Revolution. According to an obituary notice for Etienne Arago in the *Moniteur des Arts* of 11th March 1892, it represents Arago, an ardent Republican, who was Director of the *Théâtre du Vaudeville* at the time of the July Revolution and apparently supplied guns to the rebels from the properties room of his theatre.

The problem of creating an aesthetically satisfying combination of contemporary civic dress and modern nude forms in painting was one that was usually evaded by French painters in the first half of the nineteenth century, and the difficulties it involved partly account for Delacroix's preference for themes from the past or contemporary scenes from exotic lands. It was not faced squarely and solved until Manet painted his *Déjeuner sur l'Herbe* in 1863. Unlike Manet, Delacroix circumvents it in the *Liberty Leading the People* by making allegory the justification for introducing a semi-nude female figure. Yet on the whole he arranges a happier marriage between modern progress and the nude than Horace Vernet, who in the following decade placed a nude engine driver at the controls of a steam locomotive, on a ceiling in the *Palais Bourbon*.

Several smaller paintings from the period of the *Liberty Leading the People* suggest, like the *Liberty* itself, a temporary reaction against the florid colouring of the *Sardanapalus* and a return to ' *ce bon noir, cette heureuse saleté* ' which Delacroix had been seeking during the early stages of the *Massacre de Scio*. The *Interior of a Dominican Convent in Madrid* (Pl. 21), the *Boissy d'Anglas at the Convention* (Pl. 22) and the *Portrait of Paganini* (Pl. 27) are all dark and gloomy in tone. The first painting is inspired by Charles Maturin's romance, *Melmoth the Wanderer* of 1820. The setting is based not on any Spanish building, but on the late mediaeval Hall in the *Palais de Justice* at Rouen; and the monks, always referred to as Jesuits or ex-Jesuits by Maturin, are converted to the Order of St. Dominic by Delacroix. The adolescent hero of the tale is the illegitimate son of the Duchess of Moncada who, in order to atone for the sin of his mother and to save the honour of his noble Spanish family, is forced against his will to enter the convent. Having been cruelly persecuted because of his rebellious spirit, he is finally dragged, 'half driven mad, half-murdered', before the visiting Bishop to have the Devil in him exorcized. This is the episode represented in the painting. He is completely innocent. Like Tasso in the madhouse, a theme treated several times by Delacroix, he is the only sane person in a mad world; a sensitive, intelligent creature surrounded and tormented by those who cannot and will not understand him. He is thus a typical Romantic hero — a victim of circumstances which he had no hand in forming and over which he has no control, as distinct from Neo-Classical or Napoleonic heroes like Socrates, Brutus and Murat who suffer, or cause others to suffer, as a result of a conscious moral choice.

Melmoth is an overtly anti-Catholic novel. Although there is evidence that Delacroix, an admirer of Voltaire, was orthodoxly anti-clerical, it would be hard to make out a case for his being as anti-Catholic as Maturin, since he executed major paintings for three churches in Paris and many other religious pictures. It is the greater theme of the persecution of Innocence by Evil, irrespective of organized religion or politics, that appears to interest him. Never, except perhaps in the *Liberty Leading the People* and in one or two paintings where he was competing for subjects set by the Government, does religious or political commitment seem to be his primary theme. Not even in the *Massacre de Scio*.

Maturin's story may also have had poignant personal associations for Delacroix, since he was probably the natural son of a nobleman himself. He knew of the operation that had been performed seven months before his birth on his nominal father, Charles Delacroix, for the removal of a tumour weighing thirty-two pounds which, according to French medical authorities, would have made it impossible for Charles to be his true father; and he may have known for certain that he was the illegitimate son of Talleyrand and Charles' wife, as an early but unconfirmed tradition has it. In typically Romantic fashion, Delacroix often identified the misfortunes of his heroes with his own tribulations as a 'persecuted genius'. It is worth recalling that after exhibiting the *Sardanapalus* he was summoned before the Superintendent of Fine Arts to have *his* demon exorcized, to be

Plate 22 - Boissy d'Anglas at the Convention, 1831.

Plate 23 - Study for FEMMES D'ALGER, 1833-4.

Plate 24 - FEMMES D'ALGER, Salon 1834.

Plate 25 - FEMMES D'ALGER, detail.

Plate 26 - FEMMES D'ALGER, detail.

Plate 27 - Portrait of Paganini, 1831?

Plate 28 - Portrait of Chopin, 1837.

Plate 29 - ALLEGORY OF INFIDELITY, after an engraving of the painting by Veronese in the National Gallery, London, 6 Oct. 1837.

Plate 30 - BARQUE DE DON JUAN, 1840, Salon 1841.

made to understand, that is, that unless he changed his manner he could expect no further support from the Government. He may well have seen his own difficult career as an artist as the equivalent of the enforced atonement of Maturin's hero for his mother's dishonour.

The *Boissy d'Anglas* represents a scene that occurred on 20th May 1795. An angry mob stormed the Chamber of Deputies while the Convention was in session, murdered the deputy Féraud and thrust his head on a pike before the presiding deputy, Boissy d'Anglas, who by maintaining a calm dignity managed to prevent further violence. The picture is in the tradition of revolutionary subjects initiated by David with his *Serment du Jeu de Paume*, but the style is Romantic. Unlike David, Delacroix employs an eccentric and diagonal composition; he is more interested in creating a general impression of an excited throng than in individual heroic poses; and he uses patchy contrasts of light for dramatic effect instead of an evenly diffused light for clearly defining form.

The sketch of Paganini was probably painted shortly after the Genoese virtuoso's first recital in Paris on 9th March 1831, which Delacroix attended. Tubercular and syphilitic when he came to Paris and toothless before he left, Paganini was yet at the height of his powers as a violinist. Delacroix makes him seem like a soul which has met a body by accident (as someone has described an obscure French poet). By means of expressive distortion and suppression of sharp detail, he stresses his spiritual force, his deep concentration, his assurance and vitality as a musician, rather than the physical accidents of his debilitated frame. More than that, he conveys — almost miraculously, considering the economy of means employed — a sense of the satanic power that many felt in Paganini who heard him play. The legend of Paganini's league with the Devil seems to have become especially widespread after a member of an audience at Vienna had in 1828 ' distinctly seen ' the Devil at his elbow, directing his arm and guiding his bow. He was dressed in red, had horns on his head, and carried his tail between his legs. His resemblance to the violinist was proof of Paganini's infernal origin. The myth was no doubt still current during the French tour, since in writing to the

Revue Musicale in 1831 to repudiate rumours that he had gone to gaol in his youth for murdering his mistress, Paganini took the opportunity publicly to disown all diabolical associations. Even those who were not granted a vision of the Devil felt, like a Viennese critic, that when Paganini played 'a higher spirit seemed to take possession of him'.

The pictorial rendering of a higher spirit is one of the distinguishing characteristics of Delacroix's portraiture — a spirit emanating from within, as it were, not imposed from without as in Ingres' portraits. With Ingres it is the purity of line and form more than the character of the sitter that is the higher spirit — the spirit of the *beau idéal*. Delacroix's forms are usually less polished, but for that very reason he suggests more of the inner nature of his sitters. The *Paganini* is the only portrait that Delacroix painted of a living celebrity who was not an intimate friend. The *Portrait of Chopin*, on the other hand, is of the only great man among his contemporaries to whom he was truly devoted (Pl. 28). He does not find it necessary, like Ingres in the *Portrait of Cherubini*, to introduce a colossal Muse with laurel wreath to indicate his friend's genius (though George Sand was included on the left of the original canvas, before it was cut in two by an unknown hand). Everything depends on loosely knit brushwork and on colouring, and if much seems undefined it is not only because the portrait may be unfinished but also because Delacroix felt that nobility of mind could only be suggested, not encompassed within perfect lines and burnished form.

The spiritual intensity of Delacroix's portraits is primarily what makes them important for the future. It is one of the things that Van Gogh was trying to emulate and develop when in 1888 he wrote to his brother Theo from Arles that his manner was being fertilized more by the ideas of Delacroix than by those of the Impressionists. But Delacroix's range is remarkably wide; it is not always the higher spirit that is dominant. In the *Portrait of an Old Woman* (Pl. 2) he maps out every wrinkle with heavy ridges of impasto, in a manner that is painstaking yet bold and indicates a date some twenty years earlier than the traditional one of 1843. Here the careful description of the outer shell seems to him the best path to the inner character. In the *Portrait of Baroilhet* (?) *in Turkish Costume* (Pl. 10), it is rather the costume than the character of the sitter that dominates. In the double portrait of the Count de Mornay and Prince Demidoff of 1833 (now destroyed), the detailed interior of the Count's apartment assumed almost as much importance as its occupants. The *Head of a Woman* (probably the *Tête d'étude d'une indienne* exhibited at the Salon of 1827) has much of the feminine warmth and vitality that Delacroix admired in Lawrence's female portraits, yet it is constructed of ovals as pure as Ingres' (Pl. 17).

If Chopin was a particular friend, music was of general interest to Delacroix. Painting, the theatre and music were his three constant passions. (He never married.) Mozart, not Beethoven, was his favourite composer. He felt that the music of Beethoven was more stirring than Mozart's because more melancholy and therefore more representative of the ' modern character of the arts '. But he found him ' terribly uneven ' and reserved his highest admiration for Mozart because he united perfection of form to variety of expression and because his ' technique was always up to the level of his inspiration ', whereas Beethoven was guilty of technical barbarities. He cared little on the whole for the lesser Romantic composers, except for Chopin, whose work he thought resembled Mozart's more than did anyone else's.

Likewise, in the theatre Delacroix accounted Racine, not Shakespeare, the supreme dramatist. Yet Racine did not inspire a single picture by him, while Shakespeare inspired scores. He was contantly torn between admiration for the perfection of the classic artists and for the ruder qualities of artists like Shakespeare who, he felt, were often more daring and more emotionally stimulating than the classics. Much of his Journal is devoted to discussions of who were the greater artists: Mozart or Beethoven? Racine or Shakespeare? Raphael or Michelangelo? Poussin or Rubens? ' Is disproportion one of the conditions that compel admiration? ' he asks himself in one instance. ' If Mozart, Cimarosa and Racine are less striking because of the admirable proportion in their works, do not Shakespeare, Michelangelo and Beethoven owe something of their effect to an opposite quality? ' Intellectually, he tended to argue himself on to the side of the classics, but temperamentally he was strongly attached to the others (among whom he must now be counted), and it was they who had the larger influence on his art. They in his opinion were the pioneers in the creative arts, in spite of their excesses; they dared too much, but in so doing made discoveries which became an ' eternal source of inspiration ' and were often refined into perfection by the classics.

\ The influence of the theatre on Delacroix's painting has yet to be adequately studied. From boyhood, he was an ardent theatre-goer, and at the age of twenty-one was translating passages from *Richard III*. His powerful dramatic sense in painting was no doubt much stimulated by contemporary theatre. And further research would probably show that the settings and costumes of his pictures were derived from the theatre and opera to a degree hitherto suspected but unproven. It is certain at least that Delacroix was interested in adopting some of the technical processes employed in painting theatrical settings The famous scene painter Cicéri, to whose *décors* a critic of the Salon of 1824 had likened Constable's landscapes, is known to have given him technical advice on handling colour; and Andrieu states that Boulangé, one of Cicéri's pupils, drew in the architecture of the *Taking of Constantinople* (Pl. 35) (Delacroix was not competent in the science of linear perspective). Contemporary sources also report that the *Death of Sardanapalus* and the *Sultan of Morocco and his Entourage* (Pl. 49) were blocked in with distemper — the medium used by scene painters; but this evidence should be checked by chemical analysis of the paintings since it seems to be contradicted by an entry in the Journal dated 30th July 1854, in which Delacroix writes that it might be possible to block in an oil painting with distemper. The evidence in his own writings shows that he painted preliminary sketches in distemper as early as 1840 and combined oils and distemper in the 1850s, following recipes given by Boulangé. In 1860 he considered using a combination of pastel, watercolour and oils in a single picture, thus adumbrating the complex mixtures of Degas.

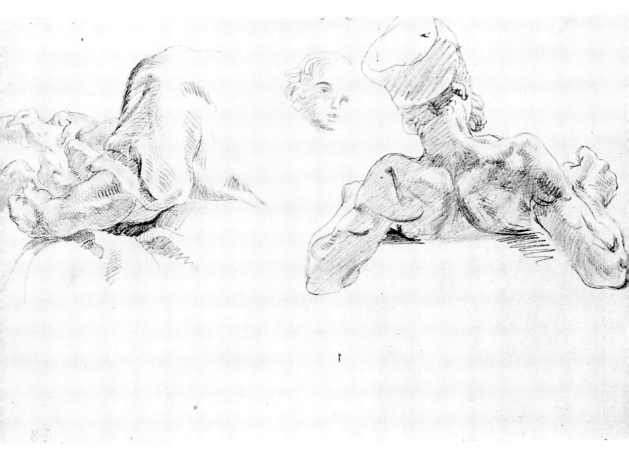

Plate 31 - Studies for Barque de Don Juan, 1840.

Plate 32 - COLUMBUS AND HIS SON AT THE MONASTERY OF LA RABIDA, 1838.

Plate 33 - Return of Columbus from the New World, 1839.

Plate 34 - Studies for TAKING OF CONSTANTINOPLE, including colour circle, 1839-40.

Plate 35 - TAKING OF CONSTANTINOPLE BY THE CRUSADERS, 1840, Salon 1841.

Plate 36 - Hamlet and the King at his Prayers, study for a lithograph of 1843.

Plate 37 - TAKING OF CONSTANTINOPLE, detail.

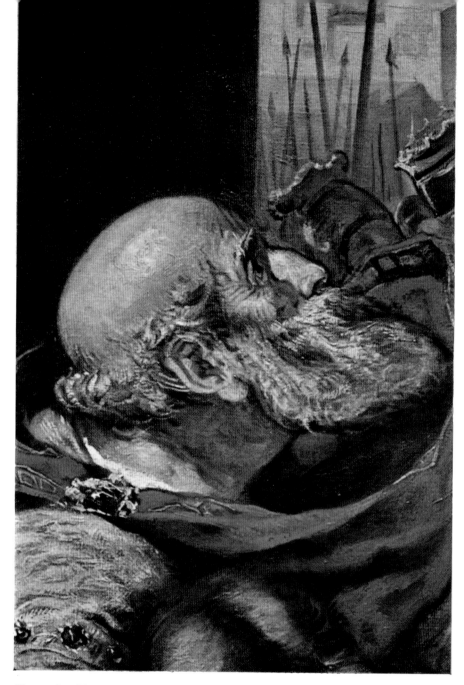

Plate 38 - TAKING OF CONSTANTINOPLE, detail.

From January 1832, Delacroix spent about five months travelling in North Africa as the artist attached to a special mission sent to the Sultan of Morocco by the French Government, and led by the Count de Mornay. Delacroix never visited Italy and the North African journey was as important to him as the Roman journeys had been to David, Ingres, Géricault and Corot. Its most obvious influence was iconographical: the things Delacroix saw during his journey supplied him with subjects for paintings for the rest of his life (Pls. 24, 49, 50, 61, 66). Also the North African experience seems to have helped him to attain in certain major pictures a balance between Romantic exoticism, to which he was drawn by temperament, and classical grandeur, which his education and training had taught him to respect (Pls. 24, 49). Amidst exotic surroundings he discovered a kind of living antiquity. Mocking the stilted classical figures of David, he wrote comparing the dignity and nobility of bearing of the contemporary Arabs to the ancient Greeks and Romans. Finally, the experience of sub-tropical sunlight seems to have sharpened Delacroix's attention to the problem of accurately reproducing natural effects of light and colour. He observes blue in shadows, and writes of the ' precious and rare influence of the sun which imparts a penetrating life to everything '. One wishes he had been more explicit, but since he was not it may be fairly assumed that the light of Africa made much the same impression on him as it was to make on Monet when he did his military service in Algeria from 1860-62. Writing in retrospect, Monet says: ' You cannot imagine how much I learnt there, and how much my vision gained. I did not realize it at first, it was not until later that the impressions of light and colour that I received sorted themselves out; but the germ of my future researches was there. '

After the North African journey Delacroix's palette brightens again. The first major work inspired by the journey is the *Femmes d'Alger* (Pl. 24), which depicts the interior of a harem and was hung at the Salon of 1834. In contrast to the imaginative exuberance of the *Sardanapalus*, it marks a peak of documentary realism in Delacroix's Salon paintings, being pieced together almost entirely from sketches done in North Africa and from studies made in Paris of costumes and accessories that Delacroix had collected during his journey. Owing to the supple monumentality of the figures and the subtlety of colouring, the picture transcends the genre triviality that is latent in this kind of subject and only too patent in the works of lesser *Orientalistes* than Delacroix. Romantic in subject and feeling, documentary in origin, it yet exhibits the classic qualities which Delacroix once defined as characteristic of antique art: 'skilful breadth of form combined with the feeling of life'.

The increase in documentary realism is accompanied by a new care in the rendering of the modifications of local colour by daylight. On a pastel study from life for the figure on the extreme left, Delacroix notes that the colour of the skirt is more red at the turning of the folds and where struck by raking daylight, more violet in the less illuminated parts (Pl. 23). These modifications are reproduced in the final painting (Pl. 26). Similarly, the blue local colour of the skirt of the central figure is modified to pale green in the highlight where the cloth is bent, facing the sunlight from the window out of sight on the left. On the top of the cushion on the far left Delacroix reproduces the effect of strong oblique light greying and blurring local colours, by partially fusing strokes of red and green while the paint was still wet to produce a neutral tone.

But just as the compositional elements of the picture do not add up to an unselective display of *bric-à-brac*, so the colouring is not merely the sum of minutely observed factual details: it is a skilful blending of realistic observation and painterly artifice. The red highlight at the bottom right of the skirt on the left, though based on nature, seems relatively too bright and too large to be quite true to nature. Delacroix apparently exaggerated its size in order to provide a chromatic link between the skirt, the scarlet slippers to the right of it, and the burning coals. It is what he would have called an '*exagération à propos*', and exaggeration, he said, must always be 'in keeping with nature or the idea'. The crimson flower pattern on the white drapery of the figure next to the negress is arbitrarily enlarged and changed to scarlet in the shadow, in order to carry over the colour of the stripes on the adjoining skirt of the negress. The black head-dress of the same seated figure existed in reality, as is known from a watercolour done in North Africa; but Delacroix invents the pink flower to relieve the black and to echo the pink of the bodice. Like-wise, it is his artistic sense rather than the given facts that causes him to place the black tube of the hookah and the coals so that they continue the black of the headdress. It is owing to devices so subtle as these as well as to strict observation of natural effects of light that the picture gives the impression of being, in the words attributed to Cézanne, ' all sewn together, worked as a whole '.

The *Femmes d'Alger* undoubtedly marks a new stage in the ration-al analytic use of colour, but it also raises the more controversial question of how far Delacroix is here influenced by scientific colour theories as distinct from his own empirical observation. Charles Blanc and Paul Signac both take this painting as an illustration of Dela-croix's scientific method, and imply that it was influenced by the colour principles of Chevreul. Eugène Chevreul was a French chemist who, among many notable achievements, invented margarine and lived to the age of 103. He began his researches into colour harmony when in 1824 he was appointed director of the dyeing department at the Gobelins Tapestry Manufactories in Paris. His writings on col-our derive in the main from the basic proposition that any colour seen in isolation appears to the eye to be surrounded by a faint au-reole of its complementary. Thus, according to Chevreul, a red spot on a white ground will seem to tint the ground around it green, a yel-low spot will tint it violet, and a blue one orange. Similarly, in nature the shadows of a blue dress, for example, would appear to be tinged with orange owing to the complementary emanation from the blue lights. From long experimental observation of this phenomenon, Chevreul finally deduced his Law of the Simultaneous Contrast of Colours which, he tells us, came to him in a moment of inspiration on 27th July 1827, while he was attending a lecture on Hannibal's Crossing of the Alps. It runs thus: ' When the eye sees two contiguous colours simultaneously, they appear as dissimilar as possible... '. If red and orange are juxtaposed, for instance, they appear as dissimilar as possible because each seems to be tinged with the complementary of the other — the red with blue, the orange with green. If two complementary colours are juxtaposed they mutually enhance each other's properties, which are opposite, to the highest possible degree. In Chevreul's opinion, complementary colours form the most pleasing of the possible harmonies of contrasting hues.

On 7th April 1828, Chevreul read a paper to the Academy of Sciences at Paris, communicating his Law of the Simultaneous Contrast of Colours and discussing some of its practical applications to the arts of tapestry, printed design, painting, etc. This paper was published in the *Mémoires* of the Academy in 1832, with a postscript requesting that it be not reprinted because the author wished to include it in a book. The book, *Of the Law of the Simultaneous Contrast of Colours and the Assortment of Coloured Objects*, was not published until 1839. In 1829 Chevreul gave a lecture on the contrast of colours at the Museum of Natural History in Paris. That is the only lecture he is known for certain to have delivered to a public audience before January 1836.

One further aspect of Chevreul's researches requires mention. He investigated, at an undetermined period before 1839, the phenomenon known as optical mixture. On the basis of experiments with woollen threads, he concluded that if threads of two different colours were juxtaposed they would, when viewed from a distance at which the two colours could not be separately distinguished, give the impression of a single colour. Blue and yellow threads, for example, would fuse into green, red and green into grey. Chevreul did not mention these experiments in his Academy paper, and therefore probably not in his lecture at the Museum of Natural History.

Now the crucial question arises: did Delacroix have any knowledge of Chevreul's ideas when he painted the *Femmes d'Alger?* The only evidence in his writings that he might have had such knowledge by the first quarter of 1834 will be found on a sheet in the back of one of his North African sketch-books preserved in the *Musée Condé* at Chantilly. He there draws a rough colour triangle and beneath it writes a note which seems certainly to derive from Chevreul. He notes two things: first, that to add black to a colour is not to create

Plate 39 - STUDY FOR ATTILA, C. 1843.

Plate 40 - ORPHEUS BRINGS THE ARTS OF PEACE TO THE PRIMITIVE GREEKS, detail
centre, 1843-7.

Plate 41 - ORPHEUS, detail right. ▶

Plate 42 - HESIOD AND HIS MUSE, watercolour, c. 1844-5.

a half-tone but only to sully the colour, that a true half-tone should be made by adding, not black, but the complementary of the colour, thus neutralizing it. Secondly, that a person with a yellow complexion has violet shadows, one with a ruddy complexion green shadows. Unfortunately this note cannot be dated with certainty. It could be contemporary with the *Femmes d'Alger;* it could equally well be later.

It is also unfortunate that Blanc's and Signac's analyses of the *Femmes d'Alger* cannot be taken as reliable evidence that Delacroix was influenced by scientific theory, because both authors falsify the colours to create complementary contrasts where they do not exist, and all their examples of optical mixture are specious. Signac, for instance, cites the red and green flower pattern on the blouse of the figure next to the negress and the yellow pattern on her pantaloon as examples of optical mixture, whereas in fact these details are, with the exception of the arbitrary colour adjustment of the flower pattern in shadow already mentioned, straightforward reproductions of the local colours as they existed in reality. Delacroix made notes of them on a watercolour done in North Africa and now in the *Musée Fabre* at Montpellier.

There are nevertheless several authentic complementary contrasts of green and red in the picture, and one of blue and orange. But since artists including Delacroix had often used complementary contrasts fortuitously, these have no historical significance unless it can be proved that they were deliberately chosen as the result of knowledge of Chevreul's ideas. The majority can be shown to have existed in the actual accessories used by Delacroix. The most that can be said therefore is that he may have selected accessories of these particular colours because he knew of Chevreul's ideas.

The strongest argument against Delacroix's knowing anything of Chevreul at this time is that the shadows of the figures in the *Femmes d'Alger* do not contain the complementaries of their dominant flesh tones, as they should do to be in keeping with the observation in the Chantilly sketch-book — or rather they are of the same khaki colour regardless of whether the lights are dominantly red or yellow.

Perhaps the most telling evidence in support of Chevreul's influence, on the other hand, is the pattern on the top of the cushion on the extreme left. As has been seen, Delacroix here produces grey half-tones by blending red and green complementaries instead of using black — precisely in the manner stated theoretically in the Chantilly note. It cannot be supposed that artists of any earlier period were unaware that a mixture of complementary colours produced a neutral tint, but it would probably have been a new departure in French painting for an artist to mix grey in this way with full consciousness of the scientific principle underlying the method and knowing that black does not exist in the spectrum. Delacroix may well have done this in his cushion. He certainly did it in some later paintings, and thus anticipated a basic principle applied by the Impressionists and Post-Impressionists in order to avoid the use of black pigment.

A full inquiry into Chevreul's influence on Delacroix is beyond the scope of this study, but some further comments must be made. Chevreul's system, once it had become general knowledge after 1839, seems to have been primarily useful to Delacroix in providing him with a simple scientific method, in the form of a colour circle, for determining the most intense contrasts of local colours, contrasts which he often exploited for decorative or expressive effect. Also in some late paintings Delacroix occasionally placed a complementary colour in shadow according to the principle noted in the Chantilly sketch-book and formulated by Chevreul. But this is by no means a general system in any of his work. Silvestre overestimates Chevreul's influence and seems inaccurate when he states that if one colour dominates in the lights of a (later) painting by Delacroix, its complementary will be dominant in the shadows.

On the whole, Chevreul's guide to harmonious colour combinations is likely to have been of little practical use to Delacroix, partly because it is based on Chevreul's personal taste, not objective criteria, but mainly because it rests on the assumption that nature exists in two dimensions only and devoid of atmosphere or reflection. Thus in discussing suitable colours for seats and walls in a theatre, Chevreul advises against the use of red on the grounds that the complementary emanations from the red would make the flesh of an audience seem green. This might be true if theatre and audience were two-dimensional, but in reality red reflections from the walls and seats would colour the complexions of the audience much more than induced complementaries. There is the further objection that Chevreul fails to take into account gradations of hue, and consequently ends up by admitting that assortments of colours which he cannot recommend in theory appear harmonious in the wings of certain birds and butterflies and in sweet peas. These fundamental shortcomings of Chevreul's system were surely not overlooked by Delacroix, who by temperament would have been inclined to side with the sweet pea rather than with an abstract system that made no allowance for it. Moreover, by 1841 at the latest Delacroix had come to the conclusion that there is no such thing as a lack of colour harmony in nature because even the most violent discords are reconciled by a unifying atmosphere and exchanges of coloured reflections. It is the reproduction of this kind of natural colour harmony in the round that is of central importance to Delacroix's mature handling of colour. Chevreul's influence seems incidental to this major purpose.

If Blanc's and Silvestre's writings are of doubtful help in arriving at an objective assessment of Delacroix's debt to Chevreul, their influence in forming later painters' attitudes to Delacroix can scarcely be overestimated. Signac, for example, the propagandist of Neo-Impressionism, is clearly influenced by Blanc in his analysis of the *Femmes d'Alger*, and Blanc's distorted facts thus became a justification for certain Neo-Impressionist practices: non-existent optical mixture in the *Femmes d'Alger* becomes a traditional sanction for the Neo-Impressionists' use of this principle. Van Gogh read Blanc on Delacroix during his Nuenen period, and largely because of this, it would seem, was to employ complementary contrasts perhaps more extensively than any other artist of the nineteenth century. It was no doubt also owing to his reading of Blanc that Van Gogh made such historically dubious interpretations of Delacroix's motives as the following: ' Why did the greatest colourist of all, Eugène Delacroix, think it essential to go South and right to Africa? Obviously, because not only in Africa but from Arles onward you are bound to find beautiful contrasts of red and green, of blue and orange, of sulphur and lilac '.

The earliest conclusive evidence of Delacroix scientifically calculating complementary contrasts with a colour circle, instead of using them fortuitously and instinctively, is in a painting whose conception and execution coincide with the publication of Chevreul's *Of the Law of Simultaneous Contrast...* The *Taking of Constantinople by the Crusaders*, which is on the monumental scale of the *Massacre de Scio* and the *Death of Sardanapalus*, was exhibited at the Salon of 1841 (Pl. 35). On a hitherto unpublished sheet of studies (Pl. 34) Delacroix draws a faint colour circle, writing the three primary colours and their complementaries on the circumference, and connects each primary to its complementary with a diameter. In the final painting three standards held by the crusaders display respectively the three primary complementary contrasts: yellow and violet, blue and orange, red and green. They would have served admirably as an illustration to Chevreul's book.

Though as a Romantic history painter Delacroix has chosen to depict a scene which occurred in 1204, the colour he uses to reconstruct this scene is of an advanced naturalism tempered, as always, by purely aesthetic considerations. In the *Constantinople* the effects of *plein air* and of real light and atmosphere seem truer than in any of Delacroix's earlier Salon paintings. One of the major reasons for this is that it is made out more by colour; and, as John Burnet remarks in his *Practical Hints on Colour in Painting*, which Delacroix read, probably about 1835 when the French translation was published: 'The more a picture is made out by colour, the lighter the effect will be, and the nearer allied to the appearance of nature in open daylight '. This development in Delacroix may be attributed primarily to the influence of Veronese. In 1859 Delacroix was to write: 'There is one man who paints brightly without violent contrast [of value], who paints the open air which we have repeatedly been told is impossible, that is Paul Veronese. In my opinion, he is probably the only one to have caught the whole secret of nature.

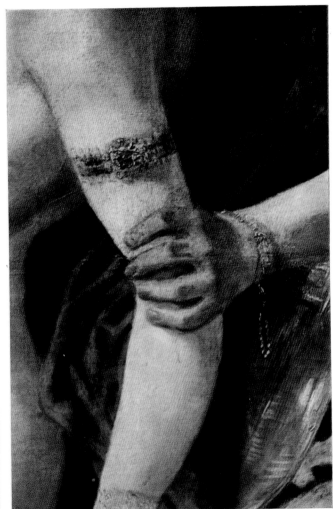

Plate 43 - Taking of Constantinople,
detail.

Plate 44 - Death of Sardanapalus, detail.

73

Plate 46 - ATTILA, detail right.

◀ Plate 45 - ATTILA THE HUN AND HIS HORDES OVERRUN ITALY AND THE ARTS, detail centre, 1843-7.

Without precisely imitating his manner, one can pass along many paths on which he has placed veritable torches '.

The main principle of Veronese's that Delacroix applies in the *Constantinople* concerns the handling of shadows. Instead of drowning the local colours in shadow with blacks and earths, Delacroix makes out the larger portion of his canvas in a half-tone which contains a considerable quantity of varied local colours. Seen in isolation, these areas (the horseman on the left of the main group, for example) would seem comparatively highly coloured, but in contrast to the brighter parts of the picture they appear to be in relative shadow. Delacroix thus eliminates academic chiaroscuro, which he considered to be a failing even of Rubens, and creates a natural impression of daylight penetrating into shadow. An instance of precisely the same method can be seen in the dwarf in shadow in the lower left corner of Veronese's *Marriage at Cana* in the Louvre.

Characteristically, Delacroix checked the validity of this principle in nature. While watching a group of labourers working in the *Champs-Elysées* under an overcast sky, he noticed that they appeared to be clearly illuminated and therefore not lacking in colour. Then a ray of sunlight fell on one of the workmen and, by contrast, threw the others into apparent shadow. From this observation he seems to have concluded that shadows in nature always contain colour, even though the greater intensity of colour in the lights may sometimes make it difficult to perceive.

By Impressionist standards, Delacroix still used, and was always to use, a great deal of earthy pigment in his shadows, but the progressive clarification of his palette as he became better acquainted with the workings of nature is an important step towards the overall luminosity attained by the Impressionists.

In the *Constantinople* Delacroix applies several other principles of his mature colour practice, which were to be formulated in writing in the 1850s, notably in his entries in the Journal for a projected Dictionary of the Fine Arts. He began to compile the Dictionary, which was never completed, in January 1857 upon his election to the French Academy of Fine Arts following his eighth candidacy for a vacant seat.

◀ Plate 47 - Triumph of Apollo, oil sketch, 1850.

77

Variation in touch, that is to say in size, shape and thickness of brush strokes, is one of these principles. By this means Delacroix, in contrast to academic painters, creates an illusion of relief without harsh chiaroscuro, of recession without linear perspective, of the animation of natural light and atmosphere. Strongly accented touch, he was to write, makes the planes of objects project; the reverse makes them recede. Thus in the head of the old man (Pl. 38), the foremost protuberance of the cranium consists of large, thick strokes while the receding planes are thin and smooth. In this way Delacroix creates in the major flesh passages of the *Constantinople* a synthesis between the thick impasto technique of a work like the *Barque de Dante* and the thinner, more transparent colouring of a passage such as the slave's foot in the *Sardanapalus*. A broken, accented touch is often, as in this instance, the equivalent of reflection, and Delacroix was also to note that in nature the closer an object is to the eye the more reflections it will appear to contain, the **farther** away it is the more mat it becomes. In the same note he records that he had seen that Rubens reproduced this effect somewhere. In keeping with this observation, the points of the old man's head closest to the eye are full of reflected light, the more distant points are mat. Similarly, in the picture as a whole the major figures are made to stand forward from the minor and more distant by their more complex reflections (see the central horse in comparison to the other horses). Although Delacroix claims that he saw this device in Rubens, it seems more generally true that Rubens does not, as Delacroix remarked on another occasion, vary the reflections on his figures according to their distance from the eye in pictorial space. In his maturity Delacroix is more systematic in this respect, and it therefore seems that Nature more than Rubens may here have been his teacher.

Touch and reflection are an integral part of Delacroix's mature concept of *liaison*, which has been defined in connexion with the *Massacre de Scio*: through correspondences of texture and modulated colour various parts of the *Constantinople* are woven into a chromatic and atmospheric harmony more complex and subtle in nuance than in the earlier Salon paintings that have been studied. Note how the airy texture and yellow and silver-blue reflections in the old man's beard are repeated in the texture and colour of his tunic. Or how the hands of the group in the right foreground are harmonized with the drapery behind them by common nuances of colour and touch (Pl. 43); and contrast this richly modulated, atmospherically homogeneous surface with the stiffer handling and sharp transitions in a detail from the foreground of the *Sardanapalus* (Pl. 44).

The naturalistic exchange of coloured reflections between one object and another is an aspect of *liaison* to which Delacroix pays more attention in the *Constantinople* than in the *Sardanapalus* and *Femmes d'Alger*, but less than in certain later works. The red reflections from the old man's mantle in the lid of the gold casket in the left foreground are an example. Delacroix found this kind of reflection more common in Veronese than in Rubens, but neither master seems to have attempted to reproduce nature's system of reflections so scrupulously as did Delacroix from the 1840s on.

Returning to the detail of hands, it will be seen that Delacroix leaves a narrow strip of bare underpainting between the drapery and the left edge of the arm and hand with a bracelet and ring, instead of sharply accenting the contour of the limb in the manner of Ingres. He learnt this device from Rubens, and often used it in his maturity to give an impression of air circulating around his forms and of atmosphere enveloping contour. Delacroix never developed an absolute rule for contours, and to the end of his career was sometimes to mark them heavily; but as he developed a more atmospheric colour style he became 'increasingly conscious that fixed contours, which he considered of primary importance at the time of the *Massacre de Scio*, were not always consistent with a naturalistic rendering of light and air. During a conversation with George Sand and Chopin in January 1841, he explained that unbroken contours are rare in nature, that neither the light that strikes a contour nor the shadow that slides over it stops at a point that can be clearly perceived by the eye. It is therefore necessary, he said, for an artist to use, instead of an unbroken even contour, discontinuous and multiple contours, constantly varying their thickness. A practical application of this principle can be clearly seen in a sketch-painting of the 1850s, the *Arab Blacksmith* (Pl. 61). The contour of the seat of the standing figure is broken and a shadow seems to slip through the break onto a farther plane. The multiple contours on the far leg of the same figure suggest a vibrant atmosphere destroying continuity and sure definition of line, so that the edge of the calf seems now in one place, now in another, but never quite determinate. In the later nineteenth century this method was best understood and most highly developed by Cézanne.

It has seemed necessary to stress the element of naturalism in Delacroix's mature handling of colour, because it has been obscured by Gallic effusions over his Romantic passion and by a concern with Romantic iconography which fails to take into account that natural effects can be reproduced as faithfully in a literary or historical subject as in realistic subjects of the type Courbet was to favour. But it should not be forgotten that for Delacroix nature was, as he told Baudelaire, only a dictionary. It was there that he sought the definition of basic principles and checked the Old Masters' spelling; but syntax and style (bold sacrifices of inessential detail, appropriate exaggerations of natural effects, arbitrary colour punctuation heightening the total harmony, the choice and distribution of local colours) were the issue of his sensibility and imagination. Even in his most objective and analytical phases, he remained firm in his belief that imagination was the highest quality that an artist could possess.

Delacroix has sometimes been accused of being backward-looking, but if he looked back to the highest traditions of the past it was in order the better to recreate the present and to prepare the future, not to take refuge in a sterile and regressive eclecticism. Why, it may be wondered, did he go beyond his models, especially in regard to *liaison*, which he deemed to have been inadequately treated by the greatest colourists of the past and by his progressive young contemporary Courbet? This may always remain a partial mystery, but several possible causes can be suggested. John Burnet's treatise was probably an important influence. While he makes unpedantic analyses of

Plate 48 - PEACE DESCENDS TO EARTH BRINGING ABUNDANCE, 1852.

Plate 50 - ARABS PLAYING CHESS, 1847-?49.

◀ Plate 49 - SULTAN OF MOROCCO AND HIS ENTOURAGE, Salon 1845.

83

Plate 51 - HENRI IV, detail from a copy after Rubens' HENRI IV CONFERRING
THE REGENCY UPON MARIA DE' MEDICI, c. 1838-41.

Plate 52 - Lion and Cayman, 1855.

Plate 53 - Tam O'Shanter, 1849?

Plate 54 - The Giaour Pursuing the Ravishers of his Mistress, 1849. Salon 1850. ▶

Plate 55 - Hamlet and Horatio in the Churchyard, 1859.

works by the leading colourists of all schools, Burnet always insists that Nature is the true teacher, and attempts to clarify her lessons with admirably lucid examples based on his own empirical observations. Diderot also may have concentrated Delacroix's attention on problems of *liaison*. In his *Essai sur la peinture*, which Delacroix had read as early as about 1820 and recommended to one of his pupils in 1841, Diderot writes:

' It is those infinite reflections of shadows and substances which engender the harmony on your desk, where work and genius have thrown the pamphlet beside the inkpot, the inkpot amidst fifty objects of disparate character, form and colour. Who observes? who knows? who executes? who blends all these effects together? ...Yet the law is very simple...
' There is no artist who will not tell you that he knows all that better than I. Tell him from me that all his figures shout that he lies. '

Finally, that elusive and much abused concept the *Zeitgeist* must have played its part in forming Delacroix's vision. The spirit of rational inquiry characteristic of the nineteenth century, which induced Constable to study and reproduce cloud formations with unprecedented accuracy, was no doubt absorbed by Delacroix from the writings of such popularizing scientists as Chevreul and caused him to observe and render nature in a way that would not have been possible in an earlier age.

After 1841 Delacroix exhibited relatively few large ' *machines* ' at the Salons. As his reputation grew he was increasingly occupied with decorative schemes for official buildings and churches in Paris, and with easel paintings for dealers or private collectors. In the 1830s he had painted his first major scheme — an allegorical cycle on the walls and ceiling of the *Salon du Roi* in the *Palais Bourbon*. In the following decade he executed concurrently, with assistants, the cycle in the Library of the Chamber of Deputies in the same building (Pls. 40, 45), the cupola and half-dome in the Library of the Chamber of

Peers (now the Senate) in the *Palais du Luxembourg*, and a *Pietà* in the church of *Saint Denis du Saint Sacrement*. In 1850-51 he painted the *Triumph of Apollo* (Pl. 47) in the central section of the ceiling of the *Galerie d'Apollon* in the Louvre. This last subject can be read on three levels: as the classical myth of the Sun God's triumph over Python; as a tribute to Louis XIV, the *Roi Soleil*, in whose reign the decorations on the ceiling were begun; or as an allusion to Delacroix's personal struggle, against evil and hostile forces, to make light triumph over darkness.

Between 1851 and 1861 Delacroix painted, still with assistants, the decorations in the *Salon de la Paix* in the *Hôtel de Ville* and those in the Chapel of the Holy Angels in the church of *St. Sulpice*. The former, which were destroyed by fire during disturbances under the *Commune* in 1871, consisted of a circular ceiling painting (Pl. 48) and nineteen smaller surfaces; the latter, of a ceiling and two mural paintings (Pls. 60, 62, 63, 64, 67, 68). The cycle in the Library of the *Palais Bourbon* is the largest and best-documented of Delacroix's decorative schemes; the wall paintings in *St. Sulpice* were the most influential, being the easiest to view closely, the best-lighted, and the most advanced expression of Delacroix's colour theories and practice.

The surfaces to be decorated in the Library of the *Palais Bourbon* were two half-domes, one at each end of the room, and, ranged in a straight line between them, five cupolas, each containing space for four paintings in the pendentives. In the half-domes Delacroix depicted the dawn and twilight of ancient civilization: on the South, *Orpheus Brings the Arts of Peace to the Primitive Greeks* (Pls. 40, 41); on the North, *Attila the Hun and his Hordes Overrun Italy and the Arts* (Pls. 39, 45, 46). In the cupolas various intellectual disciplines are represented by scenes from antiquity and the Scriptures. From the South (where Delacroix began) to the North: 1. *Science;* 2. *History and Philosophy;* 3. *Rhetoric and Legislation* (the central purpose of the *Palais Bourbon* represented on the central cupola); 4. *Theology* 5. *Poetry* (Pl. 42). The paintings in the half-domes were executed directly onto the walls in an oil and wax medium. The scenes in the pendentives were painted on canvas in the studio and retouched when in place.

It is clear from the perspective of the *trompe-l'oeil* ornament in the tops of the cupolas that Delacroix intended the ideal view of the scheme to be taken from the centre of the room on entering by the main door — at a point, that is to say, immediately beneath the *Legislation* cupola and equidistant from the *Orpheus* and *Attila* half-domes. At this point one can best appreciate the balance that he attains between classic restraint and romantic violence. The *Orpheus* is calm, restful, idyllic in mood, and brought to a comparatively high finish in every part. The *Attila*, on the other hand, is agitated and disquieting. It contains the boldest suppression of detail in order to preserve a single total impression of the Barbarians' swift and devastating advance (compare Pls. 41, 46).

The precarious balance between civilization and blind destruction is a constant theme in Delacroix's work. Rarely is the victory of light so complete as in the *Triumph of Apollo*. The bouquet of flowers is always in danger of being blown to smithereens by the volcano. The civilizing work of Orpheus and his successors is trampled underfoot by the frantic horse of Attila. Pliny the Elder, in the *Science* cupola, is being civilized when about to be asphyxiated; he records scientifically the eruption of Vesuvius that destroyed him together with Herculaneum and Pompeii. But the flower can be of exceptional beauty while it lasts: the pastoral calm of the *Orpheus, Hesiod and his Muse* and *Ovid among the Scythians* (*Poetry* cupola) provides soothing interludes between cataclysms. This lyrical manner, as distinct from the 'Homeric' mode, is another way in which Delacroix must have felt that he came closer to the true spirit of antiquity than had David and Ingres. He thought while completing the *Orpheus* that it was the best thing of its kind he had painted.

It has often been held that Delacroix's classical tendencies emerged with his first large decorative cycle in the 1830s, and that until then he was a 'pure Romantic'. But in certain works he had always been classical in exactly the same way as in the *Orpheus*. The nymph rising from the bulrushes on the right of the *Orpheus* (Pl. 41) is a variant of the *Spring* in Delacroix's earliest decorative scheme — the *Four Seasons* painted in 1821 for the dining-room of the French tragedian Talma. And the *Spring* in its turn was derived from the antique *Crouching Aphrodite* and a Greco-Roman wall painting, the famous *Maiden Gathering Flowers* from the environs of Pompeii — in fact from Stabiae where Pliny was killed.

Destructive powers are often expressed by Delacroix through animals, as in Attila's horse. In his many pictures of wild beasts, lions and tigers sometimes conquer and devour lone men or women, and always defeat smaller creatures with fearful ease and savage beauty (Pl. 52). In the larger hunt scenes (Pl. 71) they take a heavy toll of men and horses; the outcome of the struggle between man and beast can seem uncertain; one may wonder if at times Delacroix did not feel that it might be better if the enraged, bristling beasts won the day. And if one may love men more than brutes or Orpheus more than Attila, who would prefer the *Orpheus* to the *Attila* as a work of art?

We are exceptionally well informed about Delacroix's technical methods in the Library decorations by Louis de Planet, who made detailed notes of Delacroix's instructions and advice while he was working as his assistant on some of the pendentive paintings. Further details concerning the late stages of the decorations, especially the two half-domes, are contained in the Journal, which Delacroix resumed in January 1847. From these two sources it appears that the Library decorations may have been important to the development of several progressive tendencies in Delacroix's use of colour. This development can be attributed partly to the natural evolution of his style, partly to the necessity to achieve the utmost clarity in a scheme that is on high and poorly lighted surfaces.

There seems to be progress in the naturalistic rendering of exchanges of reflections. De Planet records complex instructions for the most minute reproduction of reflections in the *Aristotle* pendentive in the *Science* cupola. These subtleties are often hard to perceive from ground level, but Delacroix's concern with reflection can be clearly seen in some of the flying figures. Ceres and Pallas in the

Plate 56 - BEHEADING OF JOHN THE BAPTIST, after the painting by Rubens in ST. JEAN, Malines, 1850.

Plate 57 - Marfisa and Pinabello's Lady, 1852.

Plate 58 - Weislingen Captured by Götz' Men, 1853. ▶

Plate 59 - THE SEA AT DIEPPE, 1852.

Plate 60 - Jacob Wrestling with the Angel, detail.

Plate 61 - Arab Blacksmith, c. 1853-5.

Plate 62 - Heliodorus Driven from the Temple, 1854-61. ▶

Plate 63 - HELIODORUS DRIVEN FROM THE TEMPLE, detail.

Orpheus half-dome and the Muse in *Hesiod and his Muse* (Pl. 42) receive strong reflections from the ground over which they hover. Such naturalism is not found in analagous figures in Rubens' Medici cycle in the Louvre.

There was also a progressive reduction, though not a total elimination, of black as the decorations advanced. When the *Tribute Money* in the *Theology* cupola was reached in May 1843, Delacroix composed a palette that contained no black. In the same year de Planet notes in connexion with the *Lycurgus Consulting the Pythia* in the *Legislation* cupola: 'All blacks must be excluded'. An indication of Delacroix's method of modelling flesh at this stage can be had from a free copy after Rubens' *Henri IV Conferring the Regency upon Maria de' Medici*, which Delacroix probably painted between about 1838 and 1841 in preparation for the Library decorations (Pl. 51). No black is used in the flesh, and the main planes are boldly constructed with separate patches of colour, which correspond to the colours on the palette that Delacroix composed for the St. Peter in the *Tribute Money*. The technique has more in common with works of Cézanne's early maturity than with the Rubens from which it was 'copied'. The picture was purchased by Degas in 1896.

The problem of gaining clarity in the Library decorations seems not only to have led to a reduction of black in the surface layers of paint but to have turned Delacroix's attention to the possibilities of using white or very light underpainting thinly covered with diluted oil paints to increase luminosity. De Planet reports that Delacroix found some of the earlier pendentive paintings too dark when in place, and implies that this was because the underpainting had been prepared too darkly. Then in the final phases of the scheme, while working alone on the *Attila* half-dome, Delacroix makes some observations in his Journal on the use of white grounds. He remarks that all oil painting looks '*rousse et pisseuse*' next to watercolour, because in the latter the white ground of the paper always shines through the colours, imparting an overall luminosity. At the same time he experiments with a white preparation in an oil painting of a *Sleeping Nymph*, covering it with thin glazes. This problem of finding an equivalent in oils for the luminosity and transparency of watercolour seems often to have preoccupied Delacroix in his later canvases. In the *Lion and Cayman* of 1855, for example, the influence of the white ground is felt over the entire surface (Pl. 52). Although this is a finished picture, parts of the ground are left uncovered in the top left. White grounds were to become standard practice with the Impressionists, and Cézanne was to perfect the reproduction of watercolour effects with oils. Like Delacroix in the *Lion and Cayman*, he often left bare patches of white priming in his paintings.

For a major painting the abbreviations of form in the lateral sections of the *Attila* half-dome are exceptionally drastic, and in some of the central passages the brushwork is broken up to an unusually high degree, especially in the sky and Attila's horse. Since his youth Delacroix had been concerned that in finishing a painting an artist was bound to sacrifice spontaneity of execution and some of the force of his initial inspiration. By preserving a sketchiness and an appearance of spontaneity in some of his completed paintings, he helped more than any other French painter of the first half of the nineteenth century to destroy the academic distinction between a sketch and a finished painting, and to prepare the modern view that a high technical finish is not in itself an admirable quality in a work of art. His experiments in the *Attila* seem to have quickened his concern with the question of how to retain the spontaneous energy of a sketch in a finished painting. He writes in his Journal of using an especially quick-drying medium for the figure of Italy, so that he could execute it rapidly in successive layers of paint without waiting long periods for each layer to dry. He goes on to say that by similar means he should do some sketch-paintings with the freedom and boldness of pencil sketches. The result of such experiments is that with the late Delacroix it often becomes a purely academic question to ask whether a picture is finished or not. The *Lion and Cayman* is a finished painting, but very sketchy in parts. The *Arab Blacksmith* (Pl. 61) is probably not finished, yet it can be appreciated as a complete work of art: it is difficult to believe it would have gained by being more advanced.

Delacroix's concern with rapid execution relates him to the Impressionists. There is the important difference, however, that Delacroix required speed in order to preserve the vitality of his imaginative inventions or his recollections of nature, whereas the Impressionists worked rapidly in order to record nature's shifting nuances of colour directly onto canvas outdoors. The Impressionists would not have endorsed Delacroix's statement, made in 1853, that ' it is much more important for an artist to approach the ideal that he carries within himself, and which is peculiar to him, than to be satisfied with the fleeting ideal that nature may offer. ' This attitude is nearer allied to the views of the Synthetists and Van Gogh than to those of the Impressionists.

If Delacroix's brushwork had often been highly expressive, it is charged with a rare emotional intensity in Attila's horse. This is in part the natural result of Delacroix's growing tendency to fragment his colours as he became more conscious of how in nature light breaks up when it strikes objects, and is also due to the necessity to exaggerate if he wished to make his intentions clear from floor level. It is also, though, symptomatic of a general tendency of the late Delacroix to use his brushstrokes not only as an equivalent for light and atmosphere or to define form, but as a vehicle to convey intense emotional agitation (e. g. Pls. 54, 66). The brushstrokes in the mane of Attila's horse are what Delacroix would have called ' *hachures de sentiment* '. They are varied in size, shape and direction ' *suivant l'idée ou le sentiment* ', as he had instructed de Planet that brushstrokes should be varied. This type of emotive, expressive handling was to be developed to its highest pitch by Van Gogh.

During the last decade of his life Delacroix spent much time putting his thoughts on colour in order. Although as a true Romantic he never believed that genius was completely subject to absolute rules, he tried after thirty years of practical experience as a colourist to formulate some universal laws and basic maxims. Some of these principles have been discussed in relation to the *Taking of Constantinople*. Others, which follow, have more bearing on the late work and on developments in French painting during the twenty years following

Delacroix's death. Most of these are contained in the entries for the Dictionary of Fine Arts and in a group of notes which were made at Dieppe, probably in the summer of 1854, and published in 1865 — four years, that is to say, before Monet and Renoir painted their first Impressionist water-scenes at *La Grenouillère*:

'At last I have come to convince myself that nothing exists without the three [primary] colours.'

'I used to believe that they were only in certain objects.'

'As a plane is composed of little planes, a wave of little waves, so the daylight is modified or decomposed on objects.'

'The true [i.e. local] colour of an object is always found alongside the highlight.'

'The more an object is polished or shiny, the less one sees of its own colour.'

'Every reflection [in a shadow] partakes of green, every edge of a shadow, of violet.'

'Shadow cast on the ground by whatever object is violet'.

'Banish all earthy colours.'

'Flesh reveals its true colour only in the open air and above all in sunlight... Hence the folly of making studies in the atelier.'

The significance of these notes for the future scarcely requires comment: the observation of primary colours in nature and of minute modifications of daylight and local colour, the exclusion of earthy pigments, the rendering of violet shadows, the study of figures in the open air instead of in the studio were all to be of central concern to the Impressionists. There can be no doubt that Delacroix was their leading precursor in all these respects. It is unlikely that he could ever have come to convince himself of the essential truth that everything in nature contains the three primary colours, and equally improbable that Impressionism as we know it would ever have been born, had not scientific knowledge of the polychromatic composition of white light, deriving ultimately from Newton in the eighteenth

Plate 64 - HELIODORUS DRIVEN FROM THE TEMPLE, detail.

Plate 65 - CHRIST ON THE SEA OF GALILEE, 1853?

Plate 66 - FANATICS OF TANGIER, 1857.

Plate 67 - JACOB WRESTLING WITH THE ANGEL, detail.

Plate 68 - Jacob Wrestling with the Angel, detail, 1854-61.

Plate 69 - FEMALE NUDE, 1854.

Plate 70 - HERCULES FEEDS DIOMEDES TO HIS MARES, C. 1855.

Plate 71 - Lion Hunt, 1861.

century, been widely diffused through popular scientific publications and artists' treatises in the nineteenth century.

How far did Delacroix apply his late theoretical principles in his final grand statement, the decorations in the Chapel of the Holy Angels in *St. Sulpice?* The Chapel is in the South-West corner of the nave. It measures 23 ft. from East to west, by 18 ft. On the West wall Delacroix represented *Heliodorus Driven from the Temple* (Pl. 62), a theme with its origins in Raphael's second Vatican Stanza; on the East wall, *Jacob Wrestling with the Angel* (Pl. 68). Both pictures were executed directly onto the walls with a mixture of wax and oil paints. Their lower edges stand just under 7 ft. from the floor. The chief source of illumination is a window in the South wall which consists mostly of uncoloured glass and is the same shape though slightly larger than the mural paintings. On the ceiling is a concave oval canvas of *St. Michael Defeating the Devil*, which was not executed in place. Grisaille angels decorate the four pendentives. Delacroix received the commission in the spring of 1849, but full activity in the Chapel did not begin before the summer of 1854 (the probable date of the Dieppe notes). The scheme was completed in the summer of 1861.

The composition and mood of the *Jacob and Angel* seem to have been largely inspired by Titian's altarpiece of the *Death of St. Peter Martyr* for *Santi Giovanni e Paolo*. In both pictures a pair of struggling figures was placed on one side of the foreground and dwarfed by a receding line of tall trees whose agitated, twisting motion was made to heighten the drama of the scene. Delacroix could have seen the original Titian (which was destroyed by fire in 1867) in the *Musée Napoléon* in Paris during his adolescence. If he had not seen or did not remember it, he in any case knew it from a copy by Géricault which he owned. It was not until later life that he came fully to appreciate Titian's greatness, although as early as the 1830s he had used a compositional pattern deriving from Titian's *Presentation of the Virgin* (Academy, Venice) in his *Return of Christopher Columbus* (Pl. 33).

In spite of his conviction that everything contains the three primary colours and of his advice to banish all earthy colours, Delacroix by no means excludes grey and earth pigments from the decorations at *St. Sulpice*. But he tends to concentrate them in the areas behind the principal figures, thus creating a neutral foil for the major concentrations of brighter colours. This, it would appear from Andrieu's essay, was Delacroix's intention. It is particularly evident in the *Heliodorus* with its broad surfaces of grey and brown architecture. Nor does Delacroix always, by means of an intricate hatching technique, break up the daylight where it strikes objects or figures; again he tends to reserve his most dazzling virtuosity for major figures and accessories, such as the group of Jacob and the Angel (Pl. 60) and the still-life to the right of them (Pl. 67).

The law of violet in shadow and green in reflections in shadow is observed extensively but not invariably. The shadow along the lower contour of Heliodorus' upraised leg, for example, and along his shin contains violet (Pl. 63). It is not the pure violet to be employed by the Impressionists; it seems nevertheless to be composed of a mixture that Delacroix is known to have considered very violet: red-brown, Cassel earth and white. The reflections between these strips of shadow are tinged with green. Similarly, there are faint green tints in the shadow of the white drapery beneath the knee; but here they are dominated by the strong pink reflections thrown into the shadow by the highlight of the red drapery below it — an example of the close attention Delacroix paid to *liaison* in this work. Although none of the figures at *St. Sulpice* was of course painted in the open air, Delacroix continued to make colour observations out of doors (once at least from boys playing in sunlight on the fountain in front of the church), and to apply them in his decorations. It was but a step from here to a large-scale figure painting like Monet's *Femmes au Jardin* (Louvre), executed entirely outdoors in 1866-67. And it was perhaps not before Renoir painted his *Bal au Moulin de la Galette* (Louvre) in the middle 1870s that an artist succeeded in creating such a true impression of shifting coloured light and atmosphere in a large figure painting as Delacroix in some of the figures at *St. Sulpice*.

It has been said in recent years that the influence of the *St. Sulpice* decorations on Seurat, who is known to have studied them, has been overestimated. Yet there were no other monumental paintings in which he could have found so logical a division of form into coloured components, based on observation of nature, as in certain passages at *St. Sulpice*. Seurat divided form into the following basic elements: local colour, reflections from sun and sky, reflections from nearby objects, induced complementaries. Though his handling is different, Delacroix does essentially the same thing in most respects in the white drapery of the Heliodorus. In the Dieppe notes he surmised that reflections in shadow always contain green because of the combined influence of blue reflections from the sky and yellow reflections from the sun. Hence the green tinge in the shadow of the white drapery. As has been seen, he adds to this, like Seurat, coloured reflections from a neighbouring object — in this case the red drapery. Delacroix does not include induced complementaries in this passage and never used them so much as Seurat. But in the shadows of the green drapery of the figure on the extreme right of the *Heliodorus*, he places bright red induced complementaries (Pl. 64). This appears to be a clear influence of Chevreul and a practical application of the note in the back of the North African sketch-book at Chantilly to the effect that a colour in the lights provokes its complementary in the shadows. Conditioned as he was by Charles Blanc's interpretation of Delacroix, Seurat is not likely to have missed its significance.

It is difficult to determine how far Delacroix applied his law that every shadow cast on the ground is violet, because he used and saw Cassel earth as a violet. In a pure, opaque state this pigment looks predominantly dark grey; mixed with white it assumes a marked violet hue, but is unstable and deteriorates and darkens with age. Delacroix probably employed it both for shadows cast on the ground — as for example beneath the *Jacob and Angel* (Pl. 60) — and for shadows elsewhere, as along the shin of the Heliodorus; it is placed both pure and mixed with white on a palette which, according to Andrieu, Delacroix used at *St. Sulpice*. There is every likelihood that these shadows and others of similar composition originally appeared more violet than they do now.

It is clear that a natural, colouristic rendering of open daylight was one of Delacroix's central aims at *St. Sulpice*. But, as always in Delacroix, the decorations cannot be judged in terms of naturalism alone. Not only are the secondary passages less true to nature than the primary, but the primary passages are a mixture of realism and poetic licence. Take the still-life in the *Jacob and Angel* (Pl. 67). The law that the local colour of an object is found alongside the highlights is observed more or less scrupulously in the blue drapery. The shadows of the same cloth contain dark violet; the reflections in the shadow on the left are green. But the whirling spokes of hatchings by which these reflections are rendered are no more realistic than the dancing lines of the straps below, which defy the laws of gravity. '*Hachures de sentiment*', they create a formal pattern which is of art not nature, an animation which, by definition, is of the spirit not matter. The white drapery to the right is tinted a pale pink, which has no naturalistic justification but appears to have been introduced solely to harmonize this drapery with the pink quiver and the highlights of the red drapery. Lastly, the hatchings on the hat suggest the sparkle of sunlight on straw, as in a haystack by Van Gogh; but more than that, they combine with the distortions in the drawing to bring an inanimate object to life, also as in Van Gogh. This hat is as alive as one of Delacroix's lions — or one of Van Gogh's sunflowers.

In his final written statement on art Delacroix says: 'The foremost merit of a painting is to be a feast for the eye'. But he adds, characteristically: 'That is not to say that reason should not find its place in it'. In following Delacroix's course of development as a colourist, the feast for the eye and reason have been seen constantly vying with one another, but neither is ever found quite independently of the other. In the *Death of Sardanapalus* the feast is dominant; in the *Femmes d'Alger*, reason, that is to say an objective, analytical reproduction of colour in nature; in the *Taking of Constantinople* the combination is more complex; until finally the synthesis becomes so complete at *St. Sulpice*, it seems impossible to say, despite the increase in naturalism, whether reason or imaginative pictorial artifice dominates.

If it is not always possible to draw a strict dividing line between truth to nature and arbitrary deviations from nature for pictorial effect in the work of a single artist, it is still less often so with whole schools of painters. It is nevertheless broadly true that the Impressionists and Neo-Impressionists developed primarily the rational, objective, analytic and scientific aspects of Delacroix's handling of colour. With the reaction against Impressionist objectivity and Neo-Impressionist science in the late 1880s, the arbitrary, the emotive or ' symbolic ', the abstract or ' musical ' character of his colour re-emerged and was developed by Van Gogh and Gauguin. Both artists went a step farther than Delacroix in freeing colour from a naturalistic function: Van Gogh towards a subjective expressionistic use of colour, Gauguin towards purely decorative abstraction. In the first decade of the twentieth century Matisse and other Fauves almost completed the divorce of colour from nature, to produce a riotous feast for the eye. Shortly before the first World War, Kandinsky released colour from every representational purpose, allowing it only an abstract and spiritual value; and thus the revolution in colour that Delacroix had set in motion ended.

SELECTED BIBLIOGRAPHY

A list of the principal sources that have been consulted. The most complete existing bibliographies will be found in MAURICE TOURNEUX, *Eugène Delacroix devant ses contemporains*, Paris 1886; and LUCIEN RUDRAUF, *Eugène Delacroix et le problème du romantisme artistique*, Paris 1942.

BAUDELAIRE, CHARLES: *Oeuvres*, II. *Texte établi et annoté par Y.-G. Le Dantec*, Paris 1932.

BLANC, CHARLES: *Les artistes de mon temps*, Paris 1876. The chapter on Delacroix was first published in the *Gazette des Beaux-Arts*, XVI, 1864.

BLANC, CHARLES: *Grammaire des arts du dessin*, Paris 1870 ed.

BRUYAS, ALFRED, and others: *Musée de Montpellier, la galerie Bruyas*, Paris 1876. Contains Pierre Andrieu's essay on Delacroix.

Catalogue de la vente du cabinet de M.F.V. [FRÉDÉRIC VILLOT], *le 11 Février 1865*, Paris 1865. Introduction and catalogue notes by Villot.

DELACROIX, EUGÈNE: *Journal.* 3 vols. Editor André Joubin, Paris 1950 ed.

DELACROIX, EUGÈNE, *Correspondance générale.* 5 vols. Editor André Joubin, Paris 1935-38.

DELACROIX, EUGÈNE: *Lettres*, II. Editor Philippe Burty, Paris 1880. The Introduction contains some of the surviving notes by Delacroix's assistant Gustave Lassalle-Bordes.

DELACROIX, EUGÈNE: *Lettres intimes.* Editor Alfred Dupont, Paris 1954. Contains mostly early letters not published by André Joubin.

DE PLANET, LOUIS: *Souvenirs de travaux de peinture avec M. Eugène Delacroix.* Editor André Joubin, Paris 1929.

DU CAMP, MAXIME: *Souvenirs littéraires*, II, Paris 1882.

Mémoires de l'Académie des Sciences de Paris, Paris 1832. Contains Chevreul's paper on the Law of the Simultaneous Contrast of Colours and its practical applications.

PIRON, ACHILLE: *Eugène Delacroix, sa vie et ses oeuvres*, Paris 1865. Published anonymously. Contains Delacroix's Dieppe notes on colour. The writings of Delacroix contained in this volume are reprinted in *Eugène Delacroix. Oeuvres littéraires*, 2 vols., Paris 1923.

ROBERTSON, ANDREW: *Letters and Papers.* Editor Emily Robertson, London, 2nd ed. n.d.

SAND, GEORGE: *Impressions et Souvenirs*, Paris 1873. Contains the record of Delacroix's conversation with George Sand and Chopin in January 1841.

SIGNAC, PAUL: *D'Eugène Delacroix au néo-impressionnisme*, Paris 1899.

SILVESTRE, THÉOPHILE: *Les artistes français. Etudes d'après nature*, Paris 1855.

Van Gogh, Vincent: *The Complete letters*, 3 vols., New York Graphic Society, 1957. The quotation on pp. 71-72 is taken from Vol. III, letter 538.

CATALOGUE RAISONNÉ

Robaut, Alfred, and Chesneau, Ernest: *L'oeuvre complet d'Eugène Delacroix.* Paris 1885.

BASIC MONOGRAPHS

Escholier, Raymond: *Delacroix, peintre, graveur, écrivain*, 3 vols., Paris 1926-29.

Moreau-Nélaton, Etienne: *Delacroix raconté par lui-même*, 2 vols., Paris 1916.

TREATISES BY WHICH DELACROIX WAS PROBABLY INFLUENCED

Burnet, John: *Practical Hints on Colour in Painting*, London 1827. (French ed. 1835).

Chevreul, Eugène: *De la loi du contraste simultané des couleurs et de l'assortiment des objets colorés, considéré d'après cette loi*, 2 vols. (text and plates), Paris 1839.

Diderot, Denis: *Essai sur la peinture*, in *Oeuvres complètes*, X. Editor J. Assézat, Paris 1876.

The following articles by the author contain further details on aspects of Delacroix's early work that are discussed in the present text:

Delacroix's Decorations for Talma's Dining-room, Burlington Magazine, March 1957.

The Formal Sources of Delacroix's ' Barque de Dante ', ibid. July 1958.

The Etruscan Sources of Delacroix's ' Death of Sardanapalus ', Art Bulletin, December 1960.

TABLE OF ILLUSTRATIONS

Unless otherwise stated the medium is oil on canvas. Where the date of a Salon is not preceded by another date the picture was completed in or is dated the same year as the Salon. d. = *dated*

ISTITUTO ITALIANO D'ARTI GRAFICHE
BERGAMO (ITALY)
FEBRUARY 1963

AS